# GRAND MONADNOCK

*Julia Older*

&

*Steve Sherman*

*The natural terraces of rock*
*are the steps of this temple.*
— Henry David Thoreau

# GRAND MONADNOCK

## Exploring The Most Popular Mountain In America

# Julia Older and Steve Sherman

**APPLEDORE BOOKS**

Hancock, New Hampshire

## Acknowledgements

We appreciate the generous help, interest, and expertise of many people, especially Ben Haubrich, Charles Royce, Wilbur LaPage, Marcy Tripp, Willard Williams, The Society for the Protection of New Hampshire Forests, Keene (N.H.) Public Library, New Hampshire Historical Society, and Heather Gendron.

Except for the historical prints, all photographs by the authors.

Color processing by Chromadyne Corporation.
Salem, N.H.

Printed by Sant Bani Press
Tilton, N.H., United States of America

**Copyright 1990, 2003 by Julia Older and Steve Sherman**

Second Edition

ISBN 0-9741488-0-6
Library of Congress Catalogue Card Number: LC 90-83104

*Cover:*  *Grand Monadnock, south side.*
*Title page:*  *Grand Monadnock, south side.*

to Fleur Weymouth with love

*Upper ledges, looking east.*

# CONTENTS

# PREFACE

**B**esides being the most popular mountain in America, Grand Monadnock is known as the most climbed mountain in the world. Mount Fuji in Japan had this distinction before public transportation was provided to its summit. Now in southwestern New Hampshire, 132,000 people every year hike to the top of Monadnock. Why? Because, first, Grand Monadnock has at least a dozen accessible trails graduated according to climbers' abilities. And, secondly, when hikers reach the top, on a clear day they're rewarded with spectacular panoramas extending to all six New England States.

Henry David Thoreau, Ralph Waldo Emerson, and other formative thinkers of our country hiked this mountain and endorsed it in their writings as a symbol of spiritual and environmental awareness. This mountain truly has played a part in our cultural history.

Many types of people are attracted to Grand Monadnock. We've seen fitness hikers speeding up the trails, small children on their fathers' backs, old-timers with walking sticks, experts with cameras and notebooks, young sauntering couples, and energetic school kids.

Whether you're a hiker to the 3,165-foot summit, live within its singular presence, or are just driving by Grand Monadnock, we hope this book enhances your relationship with the mountain.

J.O.
S.S.

# 1

# ROADS AND TRAILS

Grand Monadnock is located in the southwestern corner of New Hampshire. Ponds, rivers, brooks, and forests cover the land as far as you can see. In the distance white church steeples point skyward from cozy villages in a rural area of exceptional repose and beauty. And, of course, the best place to see it all is from the mountaintop.

The entrance to Monadnock State Park Headquarters is a narrow, paved, tree-lined road that rises gently past the welcome sign, gatehouse, and into a parking lot. The office of the park manager, a Visitor Center with displays and information, picnic tables, fire pits, the White Dot Trail to the summit, and campgrounds are in this area.

The park manager assigns a small number of tent sites on a first-come first-served basis, limited to fourteen consecutive days. Sites are situated in a pleasant wooded section, and public rest rooms, drinking and cooking water are provided.

The Visitor Center offers hikers the best introduction and orientation to the more than 5,000-acre Monadnock Reservation.

*Hiking the Pumpelly Trail.*

## THE FIVE MAJOR TRAILS

About 40 miles of trails crisscross the sides of Grand Monadnock, but most of the mileage covers connecting paths and cross-country ski trails. The five major trails start from all directions.

They include: Old Toll Road and White Arrow Trails
(2.2 miles, south)
Dublin Trail (2.2 miles, north)
White Dot Trail (1.9 miles, southeast)
Pumpelly Trail (4.5 miles, northeast)
Marlboro Trail (2.1 miles west)

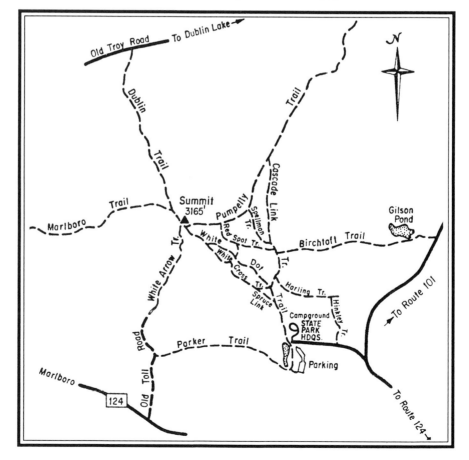

## Old Toll Road And White Arrow Trails
## (2.2 Miles)

These trails lead to the summit through plush views. They also interweave with many side trails of historical legacies.

The Old Toll Road begins on the south side of the mountain off Route 124 from Jaffrey to Troy. A large sign shows the turnoff to two ample parking lots. This unpaved road heading up the mountain is open only to foot traffic.

The road makes walking easy for a mile. About halfway, the Parker Trail from Park Headquarters intersects on the right. At the end of the road lies the clearing from the once-proud and popular Half Way House. The now vacant field reveals the rocky summit on one side and soft rolling woodland on the other.

This spot used to be the thriving focus of activity on Grand Monadnock. Except for a few foundation blocks to the side and a carved-out seat on a rock slab, virtually nothing remains of the Half Way House complex. An inscription on a rock face against the rear right corner of the clearing where the Thoreau Trail begins reads: "Site of the Hotel known as the Mountain House and later as the Half Way House, 1886-1954." Moses Spring still flows from a hole in the rock below the inscription.

*Spring violets.*

More than a half dozen side trails begin at either end of the clearing, all of them rising through rich woodland. Here, for example, you can ascend about a half mile to Thoreau Seat and Emerson Seat, two exposed rock perches overlooking the countryside.

From the north end of the Half Way House clearing, the White Arrow Trail leads to the summit. This is considered the oldest formal trail on the mountain and probably was blazed in 1706.

In 1861 the U.S. Coast and Geodetic Survey widened the trail, and, in some locations, arranged large stone steps. This wide, rocky trail can be steep at times. In spring and early summer ice melt runoff sometimes cascades down the sides of the trail. At the crest of the last steep section, the trail levels a short distance before emerging onto bird's-eye views above treeline.

## Dublin Trail (2.2 Miles)

This trail is located by turning south from Rte. 101 at Dublin Lake and following the Old Marlboro Road to Dublin Lake Club Golf Course. Turn left on unpaved Old Troy Road and follow it about one and a half miles to a trail-like clearing in thick woods.

At the outset the trail cuts through dense maple and spruce forest before narrowing and turning steep. As with most of the major trails, this one later requires some giant steps over rock slabs and boulders. It can be somewhat strenuous in a few spots, but not impossible.

The second half of the trail in distance rises twice as high in altitude as the first. About halfway up, the trail emerges into a scrub zone with low-lying brush and tenacious but delicate moss, grasses, and lichen. In summer you might find some blueberries to pick along the way. Park officials request that you avoid walking near miniature pools and swampy areas because of the fragile ecology.

The trail passes timberline at 1.7 miles and enters the open rock ledges. False hopes arise at this point because Dublin Peak appears and seems to be the summit. It isn't. In altitude it's five feet short of the true summit. Beyond this false summit the Marlboro Trail intersects the Dublin Trail, and joined together they lead to the authentic top of Grand Monadnock.

*Half Way House.*

## White Dot Trail (1.9 Miles)

This popular trail begins next to the Visitor Center at the Park Headquarters. It is the shortest, most direct route to the summit. The first three-quarters of a mile follow a gradual, wide trail through maples, oaks, birches, beeches, spruce, and pines.

One of the most refreshing features of this trail is Falcon Spring, located eight-tenths of a mile from the start. A short turnoff to the spring is clearly marked on the left. This fresh mountain water is cold and delicious. It pours from a pipe year round. Don't miss it.

Parts of the White Dot Trail follow huge, sloped, granite boulders which sometimes are imposing.

This trail also offers many vistas early on. At 1.3 miles the trail leaves the woods and opens onto an exposed stretch, with the summit visible above and the sweep of forested valleys below. After a short re-entry into woods, the trail emerges on bare-rock ledges for wide-open hiking the rest of the way. On clear days Boston skyscrapers can be seen on the eastern horizon.

*Resting at Falcon Spring.*

*Mountain Brook.*

## Pumpelly Trail (4.5 Miles)

The longest trail on Monadnock, Pumpelly stretches from nearly the southeast edge of Dublin Lake to the summit. For a long way it follows the Pumpelly Ridge through open country. Exposed walking can be pleasant, but in cold wind and rain this trail isn't recommended, and, in fact, can be dangerous.

More than the first third of the trail traces relatively flat land. The walking is easy and enjoyable through mixed forest. In autumn this section glows with seasonal reds and yellows of maple and beech. At the midsection the terrain steepens considerably. Once on the ridge the walking becomes easier. The path takes you alternately to the east and west sides of the ridge for long views of ponds and low rolling hills below.

Pumpelly Trail passes by some dramatic features — rock pools and fallen clusters of granite cliff. You'll see Thoreau's Bog at the headwaters of Mountain Brook, which cascades down the mountainside and eventually crosses Old Troy Road near the Dublin Lake Club. The trail also passes the Sarcophagus at 2,800 feet elevation on the open ridge. This is a mammoth, coffin-shaped chunk of granite isolated on a flat surface.

Toward the summit three connecting trails intersect — the Cascade Link, Spellman, and Red Dot Trails. The last mile up is marked by cairns (pyramidal piles of rock). Now you walk through gentle, open scrub and granite terrain. The summit is in plain view all along this final stretch.

## Marlboro Trail (2.1 Miles)

To find the Marlboro Trail turn onto Shaker Road from Route 124 and drive over a rough unpaved backcountry road for about three-quarters of a mile. A small parking area accommodates a few cars at the trailhead. Of interest here are stone foundations from a small Shaker community.

This trail is less hiked than others, so chances are good for long stretches of isolated walking on the lower section. For nearly a mile the trail is rather easy. Then it ascends steadily and steeply. But once you're on open ledges, the views extend to the Green Mountains in Vermont. At this level too is an eye-catching set of giant granite boulders with an overhang slab, named the Rock House for its shelter-like appearance.

When the Dublin Trail intersects the Marlboro Trail, you have three-tenths of a mile left to the summit.

---

### HARRIS CENTER

Summer visitors to the Monadnock area might be interested in activities offered by the Harris Center for Conservation Education. Located in Hancock, N.H., this non-profit organization is devoted to the preservation of the environment and educational programs for children and adults. Some of the more popular excursions include mushroom hunts, canoe trips, and nature hikes of mountains in the area.

# 2

# GEOLOGICAL FORMATION

The geological growth of Grand Monadnock is somewhat like the *Tales Of A Thousand And One Nights*. New chapters constantly are being added to its many-layered history. Monadnock represents a prototype for much of the geological activity in northern New England. In fact, a geologist coined the word *monadnock* after *the* Grand Monadnock to define similar mountains that tower as isolated peaks above an eroded level area called a peneplain.

## In The Beginning

According to most geologists, the birth of Monadnock began during the Devonian Period about four hundred million years ago when ocean covered the region. Gradually, the water receded, leaving a flat tableland composed of sand and clay sediment.

Fossils of marine life have been found in Littleton, N.H., and although no remnants of oceanic creatures have been discovered on the slopes of Grand Monadnock, it is thought that the mountain developed simultaneously with the Littleton formation.

*Effect of glaciers on south side.*

## One Great Geological Fold

After another few hundred million years, the surface-crust thrust upward. Beneath this upheaval, layers of sand and clay eventually folded and refolded. Extreme heat and pressure, sometimes as deep as nine miles below the mountain, transformed the sediment into layers of quartzite and schist. (Monadnock schist is a conglomerate of mica, garnet, tourmaline, and sillimanite.) On the exposed ledges, this folding and swirling looks like a mocha-mallow, ripple layer cake.

The entire mountain may be thought of as one great fold with seven distinct quartzite beds winding serpentine fashion from the mountain base to its wide summit bowl.

When this folding era was about at an end, boiling molten magma forced through cracks and dikes of the older rock formations. Many of these dikes are composed of tar-colored hornblende granites, while others stand out prominently as white quartz veins.

The Carboniferous stage of the mountain, two hundred and fifty million years ago, also produced colorful deposits of crystals and minerals.

# GEOLOGICAL FEATURES
# AND WHERE TO FIND THEM

**The Billings Fold:** Named for geologists Katharine Fowler Billings and Marland Billings, this is a prime example of metamorphic folding. On a southern cliff near the Smith Summit and White Arrow Trails.

**Quartzite Folds:** Seven folds wind from the mountain base. Along the Smith Summit and White Arrow Trails.

**Pyrite or Fool's Gold:** These stained-looking patches of ore occasionally are laced with greenish colored actinolite needles and other crystals. On many of the rocks along the south and eastern trails.

**Sillimanite "Bird Tracks":** Three to five-inch crystals are in evidence in much of the schist on south and eastern trails.

**Sarcophagus:** In geological terms, this is a "glacial erratic" (large boulder dumped by a melting glacier). Also named "the boat" and "bible rock" in earlier days. At about 2,800 feet elevation on the Pumpelly Trail.

**Graphite Mine:** Tiny garnets and large flecks of mica glitter in the rock where soft lead (plumbago) was mined. At about 2,560 feet elevation off the Cliff Walk Trail.

**Glacier Drag Marks:** *Striae* is the technical term for marks left by boulders scraped against bedrock by a glacier. These grooves may be identified on rocks along the Old Toll Road and on Bald Rock.

*"Sarcophagus,"*
*Pumpelly Trail.*

## Ice Cutting

The most dramatic changes in the mountain probably occurred during the Ice Age (13,000-25,000 years ago) when one glacier, and perhaps several, slid over the mountain from the north. The ice sheet pushed multi-ton boulders in its path as though they were pebbles. One of these massive boulders, now called the Sarcophagus, remains on the northern Pumpelly Trail exactly where the ice-melt dumped it.

Smooth sheep-backed stones called *roches moutonées* lend evidence to the inherent polishing and smoothing qualities of glaciers. From drag grooves where other boulders were shoved over these smooth rocks, geologists have concluded that one of the ice sheets moved twenty degrees to the southeast.

On the summit ridge above what is now the town of Dublin, gigantic boulders were pushed to the southeast side. Others were chiseled from the sheer cliff edge at joints and fissures. Smaller rocks eroded into gravel and sand which were deposited from the base of the mountain to present-day Massachusetts.

Huge masses of clay also were deposited here and there, forming round hills known as drumlins. Arctic plants cropped up and proliferated in the wake of the glaciation, and new crystals and minerals formed under tremendous pressure from the ice which was an estimated two thousand feet thick.

## Man-made And Natural Changes

Natural forces of weather and water eventually transformed the upper plains into hills and valleys. Glacial lakes dotted the landscape. Streams became entrenched as they cut deeper into the glacial till (sand and gravel). This restructuring continued at a leisurely millennial pace.

In the last few centuries, Grand Monadnock has undergone rather precipitous changes resulting from sheep grazing, severe ice storms, logging, and forest fires. Devastation from fire was so complete that the upper ledges of the summit now are barren.

However, ecologists note that scrub pines once more are seeding on the upper slopes. More common flowers and mosses are taking root, replacing the delicate alpine varieties.

*Mountain sandwort
above treeline.*

25

## The Contour Of The Mountain

The broad profile of the mountain may be pictured as the rim of a gently curved saucer, with the Pumpelly Ridge in the northwest as the other rim. Between these two points is a shallow basin. The south incline to the summit is steep, and the northern slope extends several gradual miles to Dublin Lake.

Grand Monadnock juts from the valley like a molar tooth slightly worn down on one side. Erosion has truncated and blunted the top. Glacial activity also has left a small indent in its contour at the point called the Sarcophagus.

But the mountain makes up in visibility for what it lacks in form. Its dominance as the highest mountain in the area makes it kingpin of monadnocks and lends it status as well as stature.

*Pumpelly Ridge from summit.*

# Minerals

The Monadnock Quadrangle has been called a geologist's paradise. Glaciers worked the mountain with considerable lapidary skill — scouring, cutting, and polishing the rock. In many areas, examples of metamorphic processes are in full view. Exposure of the upper ledges allows viewing of outstanding mineral specimens and formations.

One particular metamorphic "refold" directly below the summit is named for Katharine Fowler Billings and Marland Billings. This couple wrote numerous pamphlets on the geology of the Monadnock region. Their books may be found in many nearby town libraries, and provide an excellent background for geological study tours of the mountain.

Minerals discovered on or near the mountain include actinolite, apatite, biotite, bog iron, chloride, chloritoid, epidote, feldspar, garnet, graphite, hornblende, kyanite, muscovite, oligoclase-andesine, pyrite, quartz of several types, sericite, sillimanite, sphene, tourmaline, and zircon.

Graphite was mined on Monadnock at 2,560 feet elevation, and the mine may be seen a short distance off the Cliff Walk Trail. Here, the schist is pitted with tiny garnets and small needles of graphite.

*Quartz vein.*

On the eastern ridge above the Half Way House clearing, crystals of sillimanite abound. Geologists often refer to these prominently embossed, three-inch crystals as "bird tracks." Sillimanite is an aluminum silicate used for durable porcelain spark plugs and furnace linings. But most of these large crystals have been altered by heat and metamorphosed into mica.

Although some mineral specimens may be seen on the surface, enthusiastic rock hounds must remember that Grand Monadnock is a state park. Rock hunting is forbidden, except for on-site observation. Nevertheless, it is rewarding to identify the colorful varieties of minerals and striking geological features.

## Gold In Them Thar Hills

During the nineteenth century, New Hampshire caught the gold fever affecting the rest of the country and experienced a few minor gold rushes of its own. The Diamond Ledge Gold Mine Company sank mine shafts three-quarters of a mile east of Dublin township and opened for business in 1875. Shortly thereafter it closed.

*Ore.*

Conjecture has it that ore extracted from the mine probably was iron pyrite, commonly known as fool's gold. Some claim that gold nuggets were found, but neglect to mention when or where. These enthusiasts also stake a claim for New Hampshire gold as the purest in the world (if you can find it).

When climbing the mountain, the observant hiker will notice stained rusty patches of rock which may be fool's gold, or possibly biotite — a dark mica often mistaken for ore.

*Summit pool with a prominent
white quartz vein.*

| | |
|---|---|
| Manadnach | Menorgnuck |
| Manadnack | Monadnick |
| Manadnock | Monadnoc |
| Manadnuck | Monadnock |
| Manorgnuck | Monadnuck |
| Manudnock | Monodnock |
| Menadnack | Squchs menadnaks |
| Menadnak | Wahmodmaulk |
| Menadnick | Wahnodnock |
| Menadnock | Wanadnock |
| Menadnuck | Wannadnack |
| Menagnick | Wenadnack |

# 3

# THE STORY BEHIND THE NAME

The U.S. Geological Survey refers to Monadnock as an Indian name from *mon* (surpassing) *adn* (mountain), *ock* (place), or "the place of the unexcelled mountain." Another source states that the Indian name stands for *mona* (silver) *aden* (mid-height mountain) *oc* (at), or, "at silver mountain."

Yet another language expert claims that the name is Algonguin for Manitou or Manit, the guardian spirit. He combines *man* (spirit) *adn* (mountain) *oc* (place), to come up with "place of spirit mountain." However, Manitou often is described not as a guardian spirit but as a god of evil or wrongdoing. So, inversely, this could be "the mountain of evil spirit."

At least thirteen Algonguin languages were in use in Colonial America and none of them was written. Thus, Indian spellings and meanings only can be approximations.

*Moonrise.*

## Indian Relationship To The Mountain

In the northeast, Indians called themselves *abenaki*, or "people of the northern lights." Tribes living in southwestern New Hampshire settled on the Contoocook River, its tributaries, and the many ponds at the foot of the mountain. This family of Indians was known as Contoocooks, and more than likely they spoke a dialect of their own.

High mountain peaks were sacred to most Indian tribes, and we can assume that, prior to and during pioneer times, Grand Monadnock mostly was observed from below. Occasional scouting parties climbed to the upper reaches because of high visibility.

The settlers also viewed the peak with intrepid awe, and a certain amount of superstition. They claimed that they actually could hear the mountain "roar" at a distance of ten to twelve miles when a storm was brewing.

Not until the transcendentalists from Concord, Mass., discovered the appeal of Grand Monadnock did people climb it purely for their own pleasure and personal curiosity. And here we must mention the famous naturalist Henry David Thoreau (1817-1862) who was an avid Indian artifact collector and camped on the mountain several times.

If Indians had been on Monadnock in any great number, Thoreau no doubt would have mentioned signs of their presence in his notebooks, for he was by no means an amateur. He collected and identified literally thousands of arrowheads and other Indian artifacts found in his travels throughout New England. From this omission, we can surmise that Indians named the mountain, but probably worshipped it from afar.

## Records Of Early Settlers

Some Indian tribes were a constant threat to British settlers, and vice versa. On an early eighteenth century map showing the *Menadnock Hills,* cartographer William Douglass labels "a Double Line of Townships to Act as a Barrier against Indians."

In 1723 William Drummer of Massachusetts proposed building a fort blockhouse to accommodate forty men and friendly Indian scouts. Pequod Indians were retained for tracking (and scalping) enemy Indians sometimes as far northeast as "Great Manadnuck."

A few years later in his July journal entry, Captain Samuel Willard wrote: "I with fourteen men camped on the top of Wannadnack Mt. We found several old signs which the Indians had made the last year and where they camped when they killed people at Rutland, as we imagine."

Willard, who recorded this first ascent, must have been carried away by his imagination. Rutland, Mass., lies at least fifty miles south of the mountain, a considerable distance for a base camp.

*Map by Dr. William Douglass, c. 1753.*
*Note: Monadnock Hills at bottom right.*

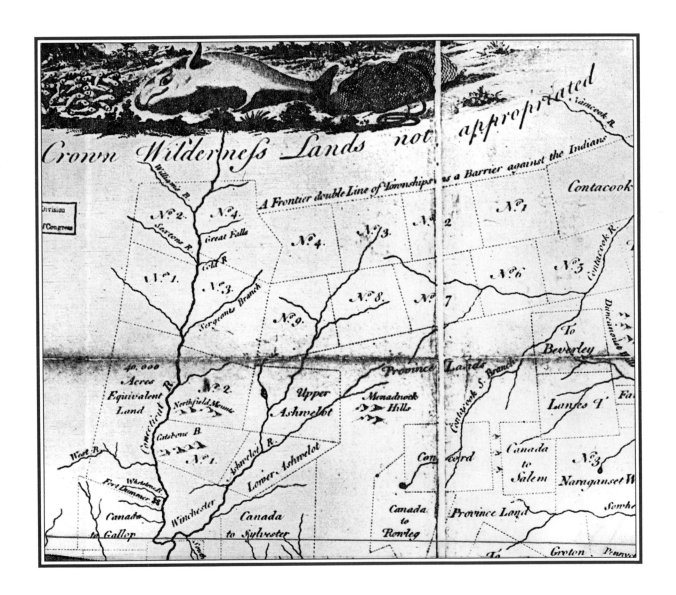

Crown Wilderness Lands not appropriated

A Frontier double Line of Townships as a Barrier against the Indians

Namcook R.

Contacook

Division of Congress

Williams R.

N.º 2.    N.º 4.

Saxtons R.

Great Falls

N.º 4.    N.º 3    N.º 2    N.º 1

Cold R.

N.º 1.    N.º 3.

Sergeants Branch    N.º 8    N.º 7    N.º 6    N.º 5

N.º 9

Contacook R.

To Beverley

Damianoke R.

40,000 Acres Equivalent Land

Connecticut R.

Province Lands

Contocook S. Branch

N.º 2.

Northfield Mount

Upper Ashwelot

Menadnock Hills

Lanes T.    Fa

Catsbone B.

N.º 1.

Ashwelot R.

Lower Ashwelot

Concord

Canada to Salem    N.º 3

Naraganset W

West R.

Fort Dummer    Whetstone R.

Winchester

Canada to Sylvester

Canada to Rowley

Canada to Gallop

South

Province Land

Sowhe

To    Groton    Pennyc

## Great Grand Manorgnuck?

The same Samuel Willard who referred to Mt. Wannadnack in his July 1725 journal subsequently spelled it Menadnick, Menagnick, and Monadnuck.

Not only are these inconsistencies due to the difficulty of interpreting Indian pronunciation, but also to the unlettered background of early colonists. Although they were secretaries in the legislature, captains in the British army, and cartographers, many of them had only a rudimentary formal education. Checking for spelling consistency definitely was not a first priority as they wrote laws, charted provincial maps, and jotted down scouting reports.

One industrious scholar has tallied up no less than twenty-two spellings for the mountain between 1700 and 1900. Most of the truly original variations come from the eighteenth century, including Great Grand Manorgnuck. The prize goes to one Lieutenant Fairbanks who writes that he's going to "Squchs menadnaks." (Squchs is thought to indicate the squash-green color of vegetation on the mountain.)

Early on, Monadnock was prefaced with the adjective Great or Grand, probably to distinguish it from smaller neighboring peaks which include Little Monadnock in Fitzwilliam, Gap Monadnock in Jaffrey, and Pack Monadnock in Peterborough.

Another Mount Monadnock lies to the north in Vermont near the Connecticut River across from Colebrook, N.H., and close to the Canadian border. Strangely enough, this mountain (3,140 feet elevation) measures only twenty feet less than Grand Monadnock (3,165 feet).

*Southwest side from Perkins Pond.*

## Generic Monadnocks

Throughout the nineteenth century, several eminent Harvard professors climbed and explored the mountain, attempting to pin down its geological history. The science of geology was fairly young, and various theories related to eras of glaciation and flood were being formulated.

Six years before the turn-of-the-century, Professor William Davis suggested that Grand Monadnock could be a prototype for all hard-rock mountains that have been formed by glaciation and stand alone on a plain. The publishers of *Webster's International Dictionary* took the suggestion seriously, and in 1900 they added the entry: *"monadnock,* n. A hill of resistant rock standing in the midst of a peneplain." (A peneplain is a geological term for an area worn down by erosion nearly into a plain.) Today, this definition holds true as a classification for all mountains with properties similar to those of Grand Monadnock.

*Fall leaves in a stream.*

## Monad

The derivation of the name Monadnock most commonly used since the late nineteenth century might have originated in the root word *monad*. Greek philosopher and mathematician Pythagoras (c.500 B.C.) incorporated the monad in his system of numbers from one to ten, which were meant to represent the entire universe. The monad was the single and first unit in his system.

Twenty centuries later, an Italian monk, Giordano Bruno, took up where Pythagoras left off. He believed the world was made up of "irreducible elements" called monads, and subsequently, he was burned at the stake for this and other beliefs.

A century after him, the German philosopher Leibniz entertained the same idea, namely, that the monad is a unit of spiritual (or physical) energy which reflects the entire universe.

Today, scientists would think of the atom as a monad because all matter in our world is composed of atoms. Oceanic bacteria and viruses are monads that form greater and greater hierarchies from protozoa to whales, each made up of the tiniest unit.

## A Unified Spelling

As appealing as the root word monad for Monadnock may seem, in reality few of the earlier spellings of the eighteenth century came close to this word. It is more likely that the early Algonguin pronunciations consolidated into Monadnock when the Concord philosophers (Emerson, Channing, Thoreau) popularized the mountain in their literary works.

They had read Pythagoras and Leibniz, and were far more familiar with the monad system of these philosophers than with *abenaki* Indian dialects of New Hampshire. The word *monad* must have attracted these educated men since it stood for their own views of nature and the universe.

Emerson spells it *Monadnoc,* paying tribute to the Indian pronunciation for *oc* (place), but retaining *Monad*. Published poems, notebooks, and essays by the Concord philosophers standardize the spelling for the first time.

## EVOLUTION OF THE NAME

Like the geological makeup of the mountain, the story of how Monadnock was named is many-layered and complex, but five basic patterns emerge:

• The *abenaki* Indian names definitely came first, and had several meanings depending on the tribe and their dialect.

• Early settlers recorded these Indian pronunciations as they heard them.

• Not until the Concord philosophers climbed and popularized the mountain in their published writings did the spelling unify into Monadnock. It is probable that this consolidation was based on their attraction to the ancient root word *monad* (from the Latin and Greek) which symbolizes a single unit reflecting the entire universe.

• Also at this stage, scientists agreed that Monadnock was a prototype for all mountains with similar features and properties. Thus, the proper noun Monadnock became the common noun monadnock.

• And finally, as far back as written records show, Monadnock always has been Great or Grand.

*The Monadnock Inn, now The Inn at Jaffrey Center,
has continued since 1920.*

# 4

# TAVERNS AND INNS

Resorts near Grand Monadnock flourished from the 1850s to the 1950s. This was the era of extended vacations on the mountain, of campouts and trail hiking, blueberry picking parties and nature-study excursions into the woods and to the summit. Ralph Waldo Emerson, Henry David Thoreau, Ulysses S. Grant, Nathaniel Hawthorne, and other luminaries spent inspiring and rejuvenating days on Monadnock. Many of them climbed the same trails that still lead to the top today.

*Hiking party on the Tip Top, 1889.*

## Early Taverns

The change in recreational life of Grand Monadnock parallels the development of transportation. Before the nation was formed, travelers from Boston to Bellows Falls, Vt., rode horseback over crude roads. They stopped overnight at farmhouses licensed by the towns for taking in boarders. In the late 1780s when commerce was more developed, cattle and sheep drovers followed widened roads to city markets, staying overnight in taverns for basic lodging and meals along the way. So did upcountry farmers freighting their butter, cheese, syrup, cider, and other products to Boston.

Soon toll road turnpikes cut through the woodland and accommodated the growing number of travelers. At the turn of the nineteenth century, one of seven turnpikes through Keene, N.H.,

*Two seasons:*
*Jaffrey Center.*

skirted Grand Monadnock and connected nearby Marlboro, Jaffrey, Rindge, and New Ipswich.

Better transportation meant better communication. By 1803 a mail and passenger stagecoach made trips every other week from New Hampshire to Boston, later scheduled every other day. Stagecoaches ran regular trips summer and winter, stopping in village taverns at Fitzwilliam, Troy, Jaffrey and Dublin. Mineral springs were in fashion, so John Joslin of Jaffrey, a well-known innkeeper, developed the Monadnock Mineral Spring House.

In the 1840s gradual increases in population and farmhouses, along with improved transportation and roads, led to the expansion of summer boarding. Enlargement of the Cheshire Railroad network and services to the Monadnock area in 1847 accompanied a building surge of area resorts and inns.

## The Half Way House

The Mountain House, an unassuming stone structure built in 1858 close to the present site of the Half Way House clearing, was the first true hotel on Grand Monadnock. Two years later Moses Cudworth of Rindge built a wagon shed and modest bedrooms for himself and the occasional adventuresome overnighter. In 1861 he built a proper two-story house. For two years he stabled the horses of people who rode up the mountainside to his clearing before they hiked the rest of the way to the top. He had space for one hundred horses.

Envisioning the resort possibilities of this magnificent mountain, Abbie and George Rice bought the site in June 1866 and opened a three-story hotel to accommodate one hundred people. Many of them took a train from Concord, Mass., to Troy, N.H., where a horse and carriage drove them up the access road to the hotel.

Unfortunately, the Mountain House burned down in October at the close of the season. In 1868 new owners built a two-and-a-half story lodging, and the hotel was in business again. The rooms and covered porch faced a cleared overlook of the long southwestern valley, and to the side offered an unobstructed summit view. Many interconnecting trails were cut from the hotel grounds to rock outcrops and given playful names — Do Drop Trail, Hedgehog Trail, Point Surprise, Monte Rosa, Hello Rock.

Ownership changed hands several times. In 1916 still another manager changed the name of the inn from the Mountain House to the Half Way House.

In 1945 the local Association to Protect Mount Monadnock bought the Half Way House and operated it as public property until 1954, when it burned to the ground and never was rebuilt. A refreshment stand replaced the hotel for about fifteen years. Then the Old Toll Road was closed to automobile traffic to insure environmental and ecological protection.

*Good-bye to horses!  The Half Way House.*

*Along Mountain Road.*

## The Shattuck Inn

For a generation the Shattuck Inn in Jaffrey was recognized as a local landmark for the choice view of Monadnock. As with most other inns, it grew from a two-story family residence into a seventy-five guest, three-story resort. Willa Cather, author of *Death Comes for the Archbishop*, was a regular guest. She was buried in the Jaffrey Center cemetery in 1947.

From the time Edmund P. Shattuck took in summer boarders in the late 1860s to when the house burned down in 1910, the Shattuck Inn was a focal point for mountain activities. The inn was so popular it was rebuilt the following summer and opened for business.

With the decline of New England resorts and watering holes, the Shattuck Inn closed its doors and was demolished in 1996.

## The Ark

Joseph Cutter bought land in Jaffrey a year after the Declaration of Independence. The property remained in the family until 1808 when Joseph Cutter, Jr., built a larger house on his share of the lots. His two-story house measured a huge 47x100 feet. Because of its size, local residents nicknamed it The Ark.

In 1873 a grandnephew, Joel Hobart Poole, bought the place. A year later a Boston doctor persuaded the Pooles to rent a portion of the house for the next five summers, and thus began the boarding business of The Ark.

To oblige the influx of guests, rooms were improved in The Ark and separate cottages built on the grounds. The resort continued operating for nearly a century.

Some of the property was sold to The Society for the Protection of New Hampshire Forests and the State of New Hampshire as the start of a farsighted project to preserve Grand Monadnock from overdevelopment.

The Monadnock Christian Conference Center bought The Ark in 1965, and it is still in constant use.


## Inns Today

The days of inns continue with The Inn at Jaffrey Center, formerly The Monadnock Inn, since 1920. The Grand View Inn & Resort, also in Jaffery Center, has updated extensive grounds and accommodations of an earlier inn at the base of Grand Monadnock.

A modern phase of travel has opened up—Bed and Breakfast accommodations. Owners of large homes with a limited number of bedrooms offer guests lodging plus breakfast served from home

*Hikers then
...and now.*

kitchens. A list of B&Bs is available at town offices, antique shops, and tourist information centers.

Not far from Grand Monadnock are other charming, year-round inns modernized for the twenty-first century. Nearby in Hancock, The Hancock Inn, dating from 1789, is the oldest continuously operated inn in New Hampshire. The Fitzwilliam Inn, dated to 1796 in Fitzwilliam, offers complete renovation of all its lodgings and dining room. Woodbound Inn in Rindge has operated by the side of tree-lined Contoocook Lake since 1892.

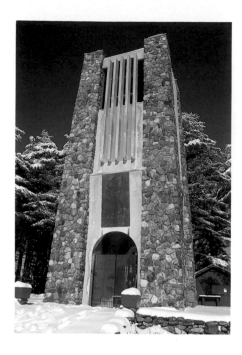

*Carillon tower
Opposite:
Altar of the Nation.*

## CATHEDRAL OF THE PINES

The Cathedral of the Pines was created as a memorial to Sanderson Sloane who died in World War II. After the war, the young man had planned to live on this land overlooking Grand Monadnock. His parents established the land as a lofty pine sanctuary for interdenominational outdoor religious and patriotic services. The Altar of the Nation faces a full view of the mountain. Set in the façade of the altar are semi-precious stones and mementos from the fifty states. The United States Congress has dedicated this site as an official memorial to American war dead.

Since it opened on Easter Sunday in 1946, more than seven million people have visited the Cathedral of the Pines.

An open fieldstone tower with carillon and bells stands as the only national memorial to women who serve the country. The Cathedral is located north of Rindge off Route 119. It presents extraordinary views of Grand Monadnock, and visitors may take advantage of them free of charge. A visitor center is open from May through fall foliage season.

56

# 5

# LITERATURE AND THE ARTS

Grand Monadnock has been a constant source of artistic inspiration. The first major writers to honor Monadnock in verse and essay were based in Concord and Boston. During the mid-nineteenth century, they camped on the mountain, kept journals, and published their sketches, sentiments, and observations.

The following wave of artists came to the Monadnock region after the turn of the twentieth century. More sedentary by nature, they viewed the mountain from their studios in Dublin and the surrounding villages, staying the idyllic summer months and packing up before the first snowfall.

Another major influx of artists arrived by invitation from Marian MacDowell as residents at the MacDowell Colony established in 1908 in Peterborough. Like her husband, composer Edward MacDowell, these artists were offered a studio and the quiet of the New Hampshire woods. During this era the Peterborough Players repertory theater company also was formed.

*Fall foliage*
*near Monadnock.*

*Henry David Thoreau from "Men of Monadnock" by Barry Faulkner.*

## The Naturalists:  Ralph Waldo Emerson, Henry David Thoreau, And Friends

In his 1836 essay *Nature* Ralph Waldo Emerson wrote, "The sunset is unlike anything that is underneath it: it wants men."  A few decades later in a letter to a hiking companion, his friend Henry David Thoreau wrote, "You must ascend a mountain to learn your relation to matter, and so to your own body."

More of an abstract thinker, Emerson believed in the spiritual

*Ralph Waldo Emerson from "Men of Monadnock" by Barry Faulkner.*

union of man and nature, while Thoreau studied nature in and of itself at close range. Both of these men from Concord, Mass., tramped up Grand Monadnock and camped on the upper ledges.

On one of these trips, poet William Ellery Channing accompanied Thoreau. Channing drew from his experiences on these treks with Thoreau and Emerson to write about the mountain in *The Wanderer,* published in 1871. Although couched in flowery Victorian language, the poem captures Channing's affinity for Monadnock.

## Other Poets Of The Golden Age

Many poets eulogized Monadnock. Their poems appeared in local newspapers and literary magazines. One enthusiastic versifier from Lowell, Mass., penned no less than one hundred and fifty stanzas extolling the mountain.

Most of New England wasn't as heavily wooded as it is today, and pastureland stretched from New Hampshire to Massachusetts, presenting extraordinary views of the mountain. Thus, Grand Monadnock was in the mind's eye of a great number of people during this flourishing literary period. Among them, Oliver Wendell Holmes once mentioned that he saw Monadnock from Bunker Hill in Boston, and poet John Greenleaf Whittier saw Monadnock from Mount Wachusett and wrote a few stanzas about it.

Concentrating on factual information down to check lists of what he carried, Henry David Thoreau wrote his journals with an emphasis on detail. Of all the literature about Monadnock during this era, these notebooks best convey the poetic solitude and overpowering grandeur of the Monadnock experience.

*In this sweet solitude, the Mountain's life,*
*I heard the wood thrush sing in the white spruce,*
*The living water, the enchanted air*
*So mingling in the crystal clearness there.*
— William Ellery Channing

60

*Monadnock was visible*
*like a sapphire against the sky.*
— Nathaniel Hawthorne

## Mark Twain and Friends
## In The Dublin Latin Quarter

Summer months in Boston, Hartford, and New York City could be just as muggy and unbearable at the beginning of the twentieth century as today. City dwellers sought refuge at watering holes along the coast or in the mountains. Artists and writers of renown settled their own summer colonies and retreats.

Dublin Lake at the foot of Grand Monadnock was such a haven and attracted the famous author Samuel Langhorne Clemens, alias Mark Twain. During the summers of 1905-6 Clemens rented a house in what then was referred to as the "Latin Quarter" after the famed artist community in Paris.

Seventy-year-old Clemens arrived in May clad in his white flannels and proceeded to write for thirty-five consecutive days, working on everything from stories to his book *The Mysterious Stranger*. In an interview, Sam reportedly accredited "the atmosphere" of Dublin for this remarkable surge of productivity.

Visual artist Abbott Thayer had recommended the "New Hampshire highlands" to Clemens, and he and editor-author Thomas Wentworth Higginson were Clemens' neighbors in the Latin Quarter. Higginson, who had published poems by Emily Dickinson, owned Glimpsewood, a summer cottage in the area.

*High Point along the White Dot Trail..*

## The Landscapes of Abbott Thayer

While Clemens and Higginson were at their desks, Abbott Thayer (1849-1914) painted the indomitable mountain from his Dublin studio. Grand Monadnock became the subject for several of his oil paintings, some of which were acquired by the New York Metropolitan Museum and the Smithsonian Freer collection in Washington, D.C. Thayer's last painting of the mountain titled "The Monadnock Angel" blends the traditional with newer concepts of art introduced by his contemporaries.

Above all, Thayer was a naturalist. He was brought up on Emerson, admired Audubon, and had hiked most of the Monadnock trails. Early in its inception, Thayer joined The Society for the Protection of New Hampshire Forests, helping to purchase large tracts of land on and near Grand Monadnock for preservation.

From the gradual development of his painting technique and style, as well as his study of nature on the mountain, Thayer formulated a unique theory of camouflage. These ideas were put into practice during World War I and still are in use today.

*In these October days Monadnock*
*and the valley and its framing hills*
*make an inspiring picture.*
— Mark Twain

*Ladies and gents on the summit, c. 1860s.*

## Other Painters And Photographers

The celebrated Abbott Thayer attracted several talented students to his studio. And when he was busy, his friends George de Forest Brush (also from the Dublin Latin Quarter) and the famous Augustus St. Gaudens in Cornish, N.H., took over the teaching.

One of Thayer's students, Barry Faulkner from Keene, N.H., won a scholarship to the American Academy in Rome. Among his most impressive works is the mural "Men of Monadnock" which still graces the wall at the Fleet Bank in Keene. It was painted in 1950 and depicts Emerson, Thoreau, and Thayer on Grand Monadnock.

Native Dubliner William Phelps abandoned painting signs and coaches to study painting in Europe. After Phelps returned to Chesham, N.H., in 1882, he discovered what was to be the subject matter of his landscapes for the rest of his career. William Phelps painted Monadnock from every perspective and in every season, thus winning him the epithet "Painter of Monadnock."

Like so many other amateur painters, Dr. Edward Emerson, son of the famous Concord philosopher, had hiked Grand Monadnock and wished to capture the majesty of the solitary peak. Seventy-five years later, one of his small paintings was exhibited in a show honoring the mountain.

Daguerrotypes and still photographs of Monadnock and the inns in the region became increasingly popular after the turn of the century. Amateur photographers hauled burdensome equipment up the steep trails to photograph ladies beneath parasols posing with mustachioed gents on the summit.

## The MacDowell Colony

Marian MacDowell jealously guarded her husband's privacy as he worked on his musical compositions in a log cabin in the woods. Guests staying with the MacDowells at Fieldcrest, their Peterborough, N.H., home, had to wait for Edward until he'd accomplished several uninterrupted hours of work. Daily, Marian saw to it that his lunch was delivered in a basket at the cabin door.

When Edward died in 1908, the visionary Marian, a pianist in her own right, presented concerts across the United States to raise funds so that she could start an artist colony on their estate of more than four hundred acres.

She called it the MacDowell Colony, and at first she invited only a handful of artists to live and work in the woods. Gradually, composers, novelists, poets, and painters flocked to the colony, and when Marian no longer could travel to pay the bills, the artists rallied support in their far-flung home towns.

One of the earliest studios was Veltin, a one-room cottage with a fieldstone fireplace and a full view of Monadnock. Poets Edwin Arlington Robinson, Elinor Wylie, and Stephen Vincent Benét, novelists Willa Cather and Thornton Wilder, composers Leonard Bernstein and Aaron Copland all worked at the MacDowell Colony and made it legend.

*Monadnock came to mean everything*
*that was helpful, healing, and full of quiet.*
                                                      — Rudyard Kipling

*MacDowell colonist.*

## Rudyard Kipling In Sight Of Monadnock

The British Nobel Prize poet-novelist Rudyard Kipling and his new American wife lived in Brattleboro, Vt., from 1892-96. The house they built adjacent land owned by relatives was named Naulakha after one of Kipling's novels. From his study window he could see Monadnock in the distance.

As with Mark Twain, Kipling seemed to take nourishment from that view. In the four years he lived at Naulakha he wrote the famous *Jungle Books, The Seven Seas, Captains Courageous,* and essays later collected under the title *Letters of Travel.*

One of these essays, "In Sight Of Monadnock," recounts his first view of the mountain. While at school in England, Rudyard had read a poem styled on Emerson's poem "Monadnoc." Later, he read the original. But it was only when Kipling kept company with Monadnock from his study day after day that he could write, "Monadnock came to mean everything that was helpful, healing, and full of quiet."

## Willa Cather

Although born in Nebraska, novelist Willa Cather (1876-1947) liked New England, and for three decades from 1917 on, she frequently stayed in Jaffrey, N.H. Willa and her lifelong companion Edith Lewis rented attic rooms in the Shattuck Inn.

At her desk beneath the eaves she could see Grand Monadnock on the horizon. When the inn was too noisy and full of summer guests, the owners put up a tent for her in the meadow where she could set up a table in full view of the mountain. She never tired of looking at it. Here, Willa wrote two of her most popular books, *My Antonia* and *Death Comes For The Archbishop*.

One year she was invited by Marian MacDowell to the MacDowell Colony. But communal life didn't appeal to this independent woman, and she repaired to the Shattuck Inn.

In 1947 Willa Cather died in New York City. However, she was buried in the cemetery at Jaffrey Center where she and her friend Edith had selected a hillside site. Engraved on Willa Cather's tombstone is a phrase from her novel *My Antonia*, "...that is happiness, to be dissolved into something complete and great."

## Continuing The Creativity

Literally thousands of songs, orchestral and chamber works, novels, poems, plays, sculptures, oils, watercolors, and mixed-media artworks have been created within a few miles of Grand Monadnock. The MacDowell Colony continues to invite young and seasoned artists alike to work in rural solitude.

Some colonists remain in the area. For example, Paul Pollaro, who has been connected with MacDowell Colony as an artist and associate director after receiving numerous fellowships, met his wife, composer Laura Clayton, when she was there. Although Pollaro's shows take him from New York City to Los Angeles, and Clayton's compositions are performed at Carnegie Hall and Tanglewood, the Monadnock area has provided a positive, quiet setting for their creative work.

Poet Galway Kinnell has been a fellow at the Colony many

times. The title poem of his second poetry collection *Flower Herding On Mount Monadnock* evokes his climb up the mountain.

Throughout the centuries the Monadnock region has attracted artists in all fields of creativity. The stories and verses of longtime resident Niels M. Bodecker have been translated for the enjoyment of children around the world. Thornton Wilder's play *Our Town*, premiered by the Peterborough Players, has been performed for thousands of people. The novels of Elinor Wylie and Willa Cather still are widely read. Aaron Copland's compositions have been played by virtually every major symphony orchestra here and abroad.

It is as though much of the work created near the mountain were imbued with a special strength and transcendence. As these creations move from beneath the mountain and into the world, they deeply affect the lives of others.

*Grand Monadnock
from Howe Reservoir.*

# 6

## MATTERS OF LIFE AND DEATH

The bright and lofty aspects of Grand Monadnock can turn to a darker side. The mountain has provided safe and rejuvenating times for countless people, but on rare occasions unexpected trouble can cloud an otherwise sunny day.

### The Dean Murder

The most celebrated mystery of Grand Monadnock centers on the unsolved murder of William K. Dean of Jaffrey. Sometime around midnight on Tuesday, August 13, 1918, sixty-three-year-old William Dean went to milk his cows in the barn. He was bludgeoned and strangled to death. The murderer — or murderers — tied his arms and legs, covered his torso with a potato sack, and carried his body to a nine-foot cistern where it was thrown in. No drag marks or wheelbarrow tracks were found.

The most intriguing theory about the motive focuses on espionage, German spies, and treason. The United States entered World War I on April 6, 1917, which heightened both patriotism and paranoia. For several months lights that looked like signals were seen on the slopes of Grand Monadnock. The flashing seemed to be directed east toward Boston harbor. Were American

*Dr. William Dean.*

troop movements being monitored by a network of enemy agents? Was vital information being relayed to German submarines?

Police inquiries revealed that Dr. Dean had asked a friend on her way to Boston to stop at the Department of Justice. She urged officials to investigate the light signals firsthand. That night Dean was murdered.

The questions asked then still are asked today. Perhaps Lawrence Colfelt was the prime suspect. He and his wife had moved from New York City to Jaffrey and rented a house on Dean's land year round. Many townspeople wondered why such a wealthy couple would winter over. Colfelt also was suspected because he didn't work or fight in the war. One theory proposes that Dean discovered Colfelt's involvement with the signals and Colfelt arranged to have him murdered.

Another theory implicates Charles Rich, a pillar of the community whose financial problems may have gotten out of hand. Did Colfelt involve Rich in the killings? Were Rich's prominent bruise and black eye from a death struggle with his friend and neighbor? Or was the bruise from a horse kick as Rich testified?

The theory that Dean's wife killed him because of his dalliance with other women is less likely. She was sixty-eight years old, in poor health, and couldn't possibly have carried the body one hundred fifty feet to the cistern. Also, her mental state was less than optimum. Mrs. Dean told local officials at the time of Dean's disappearance that her Billy could be found in the deep water; she pointed to the swamp and said they'd have to walk on the treetops to get there.

Perhaps Dean met up with burglars or a vengeful business dealer. Strangely enough, a grand jury didn't convene to deliberate until nine months later. In addition, officials in Boston blocked access to common information. Later, it was disclosed that federal agents in Washington had been keeping an eye on Colfelt *before* he moved to Jaffrey.

The verdict of the grand jury in Keene, N.H., April 22, 1919, remains unchanged: Murder by person or persons unknown.

## Plane Crashes

Rain, storms, high winds, and blizzards can strike Grand Monadnock unpredictably, but for airplane pilots, fog is the most mercurial and dangerous of all. Over the years several planes have crashed into the mountain when hidden by fog. Some pilots and passengers have survived, most didn't.

At about 10:00 A.M. on June 27, 1983, Lynn Franklin was flying in a four-seat plane from Gorham, Me., to Pawling, N.Y., when he flew into bad weather and crashed into the mountain. The Emergency Locator Transmitter on a plane automatically sends out a signal on crash impact, but Franklin's failed to last long enough. A N.H. Civil Air Patrol member in Keene only could detect the likely site as Jaffrey or Keene. Continuing bad weather delayed ground and air searches.

The plane wreckage accidentally was sighted by a pilot on a pleasure cruise over the mountain. The downed plane, with its burned cockpit and dead pilot, had smashed into a granite ledge on the southeast side near the Marlboro Trail. The wreckage was about three hundred feet below the summit.

Six months later in the deep winter of February 6, 1984, two New Jersey pilots lost their lives. If they'd flown fifty feet higher, they would have cleared the mountain. But in nighttime fog and rain, they crashed into the northeast side of Monadnock and died instantly. The impact completely demolished the twin-engine, eight-seat Cessna, scattering engine, wings, and propeller parts over the site covered with three feet of snow.

The pilots were en route from Concord, N.H., to Morristown, N.J. Both were employees of Northeast Airways; one was a former jet fighter pilot and captain in the U.S. Air Force.

This time the Emergency Locator Transmitter was locked in by a satellite operated by the Air Force Rescue and Recovery Center at Scott Air Force Base in Illinois. The N.H. Civil Air Patrol and the N.H. Fish and Game Department were notified in the middle of the night. Heavy fog delayed the search until sunrise.

Rescue searchers hiked up the icy, slippery Cascade Link and Spellman Trails. Ken Peterson of Rutland, Mass., located the wreckage at about ten in the morning.

Meanwhile, a U.S. Coast Guard helicopter flew from Otis Air Force Base on Cape Cod to the Dillant-Hopkins Airport near Keene to help in the recovery work. When the restless weather finally abated, a helicopter flew in to remove the bodies from the summit.


## Other Mishaps And Maladies

No matter how careful a hiker is, accidents happen. Broken legs, sprained ankles, heart attacks, serious allergic reactions to bee stings, diabetic attacks, appendicitis — all have occurred on the mountain.

Hikers are warned to carry whatever medication they need. Good hiking boots or shoes are suggested. Basic knowledge of how to hike is important. Avoid stepping on slippery tree roots, wear layered clothing and a windbreaker, hike slowly and surely, reserve your energy.

In 1974 an unusual series of heart attacks killed three men in four months. A seventy-seven-year-old man suffered an attack on his descent of the Pumpelly Trail in September. The next month a forty-three-year-old Boy Scoutmaster died on his way up the White Dot Trail. Then, in mid-December a forty-eight-year-old experienced hiker suffered a fatal attack near the summit.

Panic creates problems. One heart attack victim knew the outdoors and the mountain, but his companion didn't. The victim's friend panicked and rushed for help completely in the wrong direction, causing serious delay.

Heart attacks are not caused by the mountain. If you have a heart problem, choose gentler slopes.

Although Grand Monadnock often has many hikers on it, people do get lost. Planning sufficient time for the hike is important. Plenty of time should be allowed for ascent and descent, with enough extra time allotted for wrong turns and retreats.

Some people have climbed Grand Monadnock in a twenty-below zero wind chill factor, and were wearing no gloves or hats. The weather at the base of the mountain can change radically above treeline so caution in cold weather is *smart*. Sometimes when ill-equipped hikers stop, their bodies turn cold very fast. This is called hypothermia (abnormally low body temperature), a life-threatening condition.

During heavy snow years, drifts can be four to five feet deep in the woods. When snowshoers pack it down, hikers follow these trails. But above treeline, the trails fade and it's easy to get lost.

Don't let these warnings curb your enjoyment of the mountain. Accidents are not the norm. They may be avoided with basic common sense.

*Grand Monadnock in March..*

# 7

# PROTECTING THE MOUNTAIN

It's tempting to take the preserved naturalness of the mountain for granted. But visionaries throughout the last century worked hard to protect Monadnock, committing their time, talent, and energy to bring the summit and its surrounding skirt of woodlands to its present status as a park.

The seed of the preservation crusade was planted in 1883 when three Jaffrey Selectmen investigated rumors of a squatter's rights deed made nearly twenty years earlier. In a mere two years the entire peak would have passed to the owner of the Half Way House. A title search revealed that the Town of Jaffrey had sold the contested lots to Reverend Laban Ainsworth in 1784, and that his ancestors had not sold them. The Ainsworth heirs were informed of the situation, and at this point they could have sold the lots into commercial ownership. This might have evolved to disastrous high tolls, commercialism, and ecological disregard, but the Ainsworth heirs looked to larger goals. To protect the mountain for the benefit of everyone, they sold their prime acreage to the Town of Jaffrey. And so the creative plan to start a public state park took root.

*Logging near*
*Monadnock*

## Early Preservation By The Forest Sociey

In the seventeenth century Grand Monadnock and territory extending to the White Mountains were owned by Captain John Mason who had bought a British Land Grant. This deed again was purchased in 1746 by a group of Portsmouth, N.H., landed-gentry calling themselves the Masonian Proprietors. By 1749 they had established townships in the area surrounding Grand Monadnock, numbering them Monadnock 1-8, and hundred-acre lots were sold for as little as two cents an acre.

Not until the formation of The Society for the Protection of New Hampshire Forests in 1901 was the role of preservation brought to the forefront. The encroachment of a sawmill on the mountain slope resulting in the logging of two hundred acres led to the organization of the Monadnock Forestry Association in 1904. This Association petitioned the state to purchase the property in question "for the public good." The state did, establishing Monadnock State Park, which became a major safeguard in the protection of the entire mountain, not just parts of it.

Also early in the twentieth century, nearly a hundred living heirs of the original Masonian Proprietors were convinced to give over their land holdings on the mountain to the Forest Society. By 1935 private land totalling 2,675 acres had been entrusted to the Forest Society, the State of New Hampshire, and Dublin and Jaffrey Townships for public use.

## Protection Today

In recent years the Forest Society has stressed an easement program among landowner near the mountain. These conservation easements keep the land in private ownership while protecting it against future development. Approximately 12,000 private and state-owned acres are protected by easements.

Three public agencies own the twenty-seven lots of the Monadnock Reservation — the Forest Society (3,841 acres), State of New Hampshire (1,129 acres), and the town of Jaffrey (336 acres). Four of the five major trails to the summit lie completely within public ownership. The exception is the bottom half of the Pumpelly Trail, which crosses private land.

The Forest Society and the N.H. State Division of Parks operate a Visitor Center at the park enterance. Originally called the Ecocenter (many people thought it was Echo Center), this cabin includes displays of rock formations, wildlife and plantlife, and historical information. A self-guiding nature trail begins at the Center too.

*If you're going to use anything as a role model for how you protect other good things, Monadnock is the best example.*

— Paul Bofinger, President/Forester
Forest Society

# 8

# WILDFIRE, WOLVES AND WILDFLOWERS

The flora of Grand Monadnock constantly changes because of fluctuating climatic conditions and geological developments. Ordinarily, a mountain of only 3,165 feet elevation would not be considered an alpine environment. But severe denuding of the mountain by fires during the nineteenth and early twentieth centuries has bared it to conditions similar to the period of glaciation, and many high altitude species proliferate on the summit.

Animals also respond to the wiles of nature and the wills of man. Early homesteading and farming produced an environment less conducive to predatory animals and more amenable to beaver, skunk, rabbit, and deer.

Now, once again, the upper slopes are reverting to forest, and as they do, alpine flowers are disappearing to make way for other species. In addition, fox and bobcat have been seen in the area as hares and grouse return.

*Pastureland on
the Dublin Road.*

## Natural And Man-made Fires

A forest fire in 1800 smoldered for two weeks on Monadnock, consuming many soil nutrients and toppling shallow-rooted spruce and hemlock. The tangled, umbrella-shaped root systems provided excellent dens for wolves and bear already living in great number on the upper ledges. These animals had been a constant problem for sheep farmers tending pastures at the foot of the mountain.

When it was clear that the predators were multiplying, the farmers decided to set a fire and smoke them out. This fire soon blazed out of control, completely destroying most of the growth on the summit. That which did remain was destroyed a few years later by the hurricane of 1815.

In 1903, more than two hundred thousand acres of forest were lost to fire in New Hampshire. Because of this devastating loss, a fire watch was established, and in 1911 a fire warden's cabin was built on Grand Monadnock. William Falconer, the fulltime

*Bluebead lilies.*

watchman, lived in a cabin near Falcon Spring on what is now the White Dot Trail. He climbed the summit daily to look for fires. This system was discontinued in 1948, and the shelter and watch tower were dismantled in the 1950s. Aerial surveillance and better equipped fire towers in the region were then used.

*Former shelter and watch tower on summit.*

## Wolves

Timber wolf pelts from trapping and hunting commanded a handsome bounty — twenty dollars each to be collected at the nearest tavern. In those days, twenty dollars was a good incentive to pursue the wolves. Besides, they were killing farmers' sheep.

The last hunt for one tenacious wolf took place in 1820 and lasted more than a week. Several dozen men from Jaffrey and Rindge joined the hunt. The lone wolf killed a sheep right under the hunters' noses while they were getting some sleep in order to continue the hunt. Enraged, the farmers fanned out in a human chain, using bloodhounds to track its scent.

The wolf was shot on a Sunday, and church services were abandoned for a rousing celebration accompanied, one would imagine, with a few choice barrels of rum.

No more wolves were sighted on the mountain.

## Sheep

New Hampshire, Massachusetts, and Vermont were sheep country. Woolen and textile mills dominated the New England countryside. And since wolves, foxes, and fishers were animals *non grata*, most of them were eradicated. Denuded Grand Monadnock provided ideal grazing land for large flocks of sheep and some cattle.

Naturalist Henry David Thoreau took copious notes on the flora and fauna of the mountain during the mid-1800s. He mentions blueberries, bunchberries, choke cherries, mountain cranberries, viburnum and other scrub-type plants that grew in the wake of fire. He notes predatory birds like the nighthawk, and lists commoner birds living in the sparse spruce on the upper ledges. An insatiable observer, he details the microcosm of small ponds on the summit, and wonders how the peepers came to live "in such high status."

But the larger animals seem to be missing from his journals. Evidently, little cover remained to protect them, and few animals could find safe refuge on the barren upper ledges.

*Eft.*

## Snakes And Spiders

Hikers and campers at Monadnock State Park probably will be wondering about poisonous snakes and spiders. Fortunately, New Hampshire is blessed with benign reptiles and arachnids (mites, ticks and spiders).

Hikers climbing in the spring probably will see colorful newts, efts, and salamanders on or near the trails. All summer long, ringneck, red-bellied, brown and green snakes sun on rocks and ledges. They are harmless and quite as afraid of humans as some humans are of them. Snapping turtles as large as iron frying pans have been spotted in the primeval ooze of swamps at the base of Grand Monadnock.

Roadside patches of poison ivy proliferate, and ragweed and goldenrod pollinate from mid-July through September.

Southern New Hampshire isn't tick country. However, to be on the safe side, sit on a jacket or other ground cover, and wear socks when hiking. Lyme disease, a debilitating infection carried by some ticks in areas of New England, has been spreading.

Black flies and no-see-ums swarm from the damp earth from early April through mid-June, when the mosquitoes take over. During these months it's best to climb on sunny, breezy days.

## Birds

Records of bird life on and around Monadnock are long-standing. Abbott Thayer, Dublin artist and naturalist, published original essays on animal coloration and camouflage. His son Gerald followed his father's interests and made his own contributions, noting that various warbler species make niches for themselves at different elevations, thus lessening food and nesting competition. Gerald Thayer published a list of one hundred and seventy-nine bird species he had observed in the Dublin region during the early 1900s.

Elliott and Kathleen Allison also extensively studied birds in the Dublin area. Their publication, *Monadnock Sightings— Birds of Dublin, N.H. 1909-1979,* compared Thayer's earlier list with more recent findings. The Allisons were first to list turkey vultures. Open landfills and dumps are cited for attracting vultures, gulls, raccoon and opposums to the region.

Rick Youst of Antioch New England Graduate School has compiled a list for the Forest Society which includes one hundred and eighty-seven species sighted on or near Grand Monadnock.

*Mallards.*  91

# The Four Seasons

Many of the trails are impassable during the stormy winter and very early spring. Still, on a sunny April day, the mountain can be most magical with constant water trilling and spilling off the icy ledges. In the woods, May flowers are just poking through the decayed leaves, along with trillium, Indian pipes, and violets. Toward the summit, wet rock façades glisten in the sunlight, and a sharp tangy odor of spruce permeates the air. Juncos, which seem to thrive on cold weather, hop and skim along the slushy trail. Apricot and raspberry colored azaleas bloom near the clear summit pools.

By June the beech and birch have fanned into cool, dappled canopies, and fiddlehead ferns nearly are unfurled. Choke cherry petals litter the ground, and the waxy leaves of trout lilies dot the banks of springs and rivulets. Spring warblers give way to the larger, noisy towhees and catbirds. At dusk the hermit thrushes sing their cascading lullabies.

By July and August the mountaintop is asizzle. Bracken and fern fill the air with a strong pungency, and sweet, winey blueberries on the outcrops offer hikers a tantalizing treat.

Vultures soar the updrafts as hot air currents rise from the steamy tableland. In the cool of the forest, chipmunks sit on boulders and scold passing hikers. Berries form on the May flowers, trillium, and wintergreen plants. The water dries up, and colorful green and brown snakes slither along dry creek beds and culverts.

*Clockwise from top left:*
*Summer, Perkins Pond.*
*Fall, White Dot Trail.*
*Winter, Park entrance.*
*Spring, Old Toll Road.*

Fall brings goldenrod and asters. The beech leaves turn golden, and then pale and papery. Mushrooms show teeth marks from nibbling chipmunks and red squirrels. Hemlock and spruce needles and cones are blown off by wintry blasts of wind. Hawks soar the thermals. Mountain cranberries ripen to brilliant scarlet, and sumac spikes burn like torches. Sugar and swamp maples, ignited by the first frost, flame into orange and red. By Columbus Day in October, this glowing spectacle is mirrored in every lake and pond.

The aftermath of this autumnal conflagration brings a somber dirge of greys and browns. With their cover blown away, porcupine, beaver, and white-tailed deer come out to feed mostly at dawn and dusk.

November brings truckloads of hunters. Wild turkey (successfully reintroduced to the area by the N.H. Fish and Game Department) flock through the stark woods. Mallards and pintail ducks circle the pristine lakes one last time and head south. The great blue herons flap their giant wings and head for warmer climates.

Left behind, chickadees and blue jays chatter from snow-dusted spruce and hemlock boughs. The red cap of a woodpecker flashes for an instant and is gone. The night sky turns clear and sharp, and silence is profound.

Once more Grand Monadnock returns to the cold deep quiescence of winter.

*Tent site, Monadnock State Park.*

*A great lookout!*

# 9

# VIEWPOINTS

**E**ach person has a different viewpoint of Grand Monadnock. The following observations by people who have a variety of relationships to the mountain show the wide scope of interest Monadnock engenders. For example, Ken Peterson has hiked it nearly one thousand times. Dianne Enos and her Monadnock Dance Ensemble perform their tribute to the mountain on the summit each autumn. Paul Bofinger with the Forest Sociaty works behind the scenes to negotiate its continued protection. Although the perspectives are different, an obvious affection for the peak that stands alone comes through in these personal statements.

*Summer Crowds.*

## Wilbur LaPage
## Director, N.H. Parks And Recreation

"I grew up on the slopes of Monadnock. I spent all my spare time up there. And when I was old enough I worked there, first with the old Half Way House and then a state job when I was sixteen years old, working on the summit and the trails.

"I went to college and ended up being one of the first federally employed researchers on outdoor recreation, studying the impact of people on their environment. I retired after twenty-five years, taught at the University of New Hampshire, and then took this job. Looking back, in every instance I can see a direct thread to those early years on Monadnock and the lessons it teaches.

"I dedicated a book of poems to Monadnock. It's a light-hearted mountain. There are a lot of people on it, a lot of voices, a lot of life. It's very heavily climbed, and very heavily loved.

"After reading Thoreau I wanted to find his exact campsites. I took his journals and went looking. I found them and was able to spend the night on the mountain. Somewhere in his writings Thoreau makes the comment, this may not be the exact quote, 'Although it is true that I never did anything materially to assist the sun to rise, I never doubted the absolute necessity of my being present for the event.' I wanted to see what he meant by seeing the sunrise from Monadnock.

"The mountain sensitizes people in the essentiality of nature in our lives — getting wet from blueberry bushes along the trail, walking in the early morning at higher altitudes. Monadnock is a teacher in a very gentle way."

## Ben Haubrich
## Manager, Monadnock State Park

"I sometimes go up when I want to think about things. Every week there's something always a little bit different — the wildlife, the weather, the vegetation, the flowers in bloom. I really do like to go up in the spring too, but winter can be just a beautiful time to hike if it's a sunny day with good snow, the temperature in the twenties, the snow hard-packed on the trails, and it's blanketed white. Monadnock will always have a strong place in my life.

"I've laid out a lot of cross-country ski trails since I've been manager. The trails are generally at the base and they're all mapped out.

"There's been a moose on the mountain for the past six weeks, and we've had some bear sightings and bobcat too. There have been a lot more animals on the mountain since pets were banned. Dogs especially frighten wildlife.

"A big difference between Monadnock and other mountains is that we're closer to population centers, which is why we're so busy. Also, it's a relatively easy mountain to climb.

"I was at Camels Hump in Vermont, the most popular mountain in that state, when a volunteer was explaining that about ten thousand people hike it every year. I told him that I work at Mount Monadnock and we were expecting ten thousand people next weekend for the fall colors!"

*Dianne Eno .*
*Opposite: Summit dance.*

### Dianne Eno
### Artistic Director, The Monadnock Dance Ensemble

"I'm a lifelong resident of the Monadnock area. I grew up hiking to the summit. I've also been dancing since I was three years old, so it was only natural that these two facets eventually joined together — Mount Monadnock and dancing.

"We call our performance the Mount Monadnock Celebration of Dance. We've performed on the summit for the last five years, and now every fall hundreds of people climb up to see our work. It is an environmentally-inspired modern dance performance which we hope rekindles an appreciation of the mountain.

"Last year we presented seven dances, and each of them was specifically created for the summit. In fact, each dance was inspired by the beauty and natural history that makes Monadnock so special.

"This Celebration of Dance evolved to where I became an environmentally-concerned choreographer. I'm trying not to force my art superficially onto the summit rocks. I want to mold life experience, artistic vision, and the human form with Monadnock. I know for me it has become the truest form of artistic expression."

*It's very heavily climbed*
*and very heavily loved.*

— Wilbur Lapage, Director
N.H. Parks and Recreation

## Larry Davis
## Summit Hiker 365 Consecutive Days

"I actually didn't realize I was going to attempt hiking Monadnock every day until I'd already started. Then a few people hinted — you know, nobody has tried to do it every day. The idea just kind of developed, like an avalanche.

"My specialty is to wait until the weather is really *bad* and then go out. I like to see the extreme part of what goes on around here when everybody hides from it. If it's really bad, good.

"I've gone on all the trails, and in between. My schedule is that I'm sticking to the main trail from the Park Headquarters — the White Dot Trail — because it's quick. I'm on the mountain pretty much the same time every day — about noon.

"The mountain has always treated me really good. I get what I want when I'm there. I'm outdoors, I like the weather, the nature part of it. As far as being in shape, I have to give a little credit to my mountain. I'm beginning to know what it's like to *not* go a day without it. Monadnock's kind of my home away from home."

## Ken Peterson
## Summit Hiker 1,000 Times

"I'm averaging two hundred climbs a year now. I keep track of every climb, the dates and notes on them. I'd like to do one thousand with an exact record.

"Winter is primarily when I do most of my climbs. But in summer I patrol for the state and usually hang around on the summit weekends answering questions and helping out if any problems come up. In winter I'll do three or four climbs a day.

"Actually, it's easier to climb in winter. The soft snow makes a very low impact on your legs; in summer you're pounding on rocks. You don't need snowshoes on Monadnock, just occasionally in a heavy storm, because the main trails get tracked out real quick. In eight hundred climbs I've used snowshoes maybe three or four times.

"I average one sprained ankle a year. It's foolishness — running on the trail or trying to make time.

"I've hiked all forty-eight 4,000-footers up north, and I was wondering if I'd enjoy Monadnock after climbing all those peaks up there. But I enjoy Monadnock more than ever."

*Monadnock's kind of my home away from home.*

— Larry Davis
Summit Hiker

## Carrol Tenney
## Holistic Health Counselor

"All the sacred places all over the earth have ley lines [energy channels] connecting them. There are four and a half ley lines on top of Mount Monadnock, and that's a lot. They mark Monadnock as a center in that respect.

"Some Sioux Indians from Dakota came east at the time of the Harmonic Convergence [August 16-17, 1987, culmination of a Mayan cycle] and did sacred ceremonies because they heard that Monadnock was the Gateway to the East. Godfrey and Charles Chips came for the ceremonies. This is the most important mountain on the East Coast, which is interesting because the highest mountain in the East is in Virginia, and the White Mountains are higher. But Monadnock is the sacred one.

"There are many healing centers around Monadnock, including the Monadnock Clinic where I work, plus the Monadnock Bible Center, the Dublin Christian Academy, the Marathon House, Beech Hill, and others. The mountain seems to attract a lot of holistic health care. It's said in Dublin that you come there to heal or be healed.

"Quite a few shoebox shaped stone chambers are located around the mountain. Some people say they date from 10,000 B.C. They're very similar to structures built by the Stonehenge people in England. About two hundred of them are all over New England, especially along the Connecticut River. Several in Putney face Monadnock. Also, some people think that Monadnock was an Atlantean healing temple."

*Chapel at Stone Pond.*

## Charles Royce
## Manager, Monadnock State Park 1961-72

"The mountain is special geographically, being a monadnock. It's unique in the sense that it isn't a Mt. Adams or a Mt. Washington. You climb those and look right onto another mountain.

"I've seen more good than bad changes over the years. What I hope is that we have good caretakers, that we preserve and protect what we have in not commercializing the mountain too much. I've had people ask me, for example, why we don't mark Thoreau's three campsites on Monadnock. I say that if they're really interested, they'll go find the sites. We don't want to have a neon sign saying, 'Here's the spot.'

"I think the Marlboro and Dublin Trails should be left kind of basic and primitive rather than putting in parking lots and improving the roads to them.

"There are very few Indian artifacts or information of Indians on the mountain itself. But once an arrowhead was found on the Cascade Link Trail at the base of a tree. The person was hiking, sat down to rest, poked around with a stick, and turned up an arrowhead, which is very unusual because the periphery of Monadnock wasn't used much by Indians for encampments or hunting grounds.

"I've never known of any other artifacts found on Monadnock, and historically my family goes back in Jaffrey to the 1820s; my grandfather helped lay out the White Dot Trail. The Indians observed Monadnock from a distance. They revered it."

## Paul Bofinger
## President/Forester
## Society For The Protection Of N.H. Forests

"Monadnock is like the heart of the Forest Society. The soul may be the White Mountains, but the heart, the working organ, is Monadnock.

"It's a very special piece of New Hampshire landscape. You don't save a mountain like Monadnock and provide continued public access without involving the local town government, private landowners, the state, and private organizations such as the Society. You really need all of them working together. Monadnock probably never will be finished being protected.

"We went through an era in the 1890s and the early 1900s when virtually everybody who really loved the mountain felt they had to create their own trail. Let's face it. They did! But I think we can be thankful that at all four points on the compass there still are places for people to get away from the crowds — if they look at the map.

"And you don't always have to go to the summit. Maybe that's another good thing about Monadnock — that it's not reaching the summit that only gives you a sense of achievement. You can go halfway up for a view or a different natural environment to get a sense of peace and an understanding of the area."

*Every morning*
*I look out the front door*
*to see if Mount Monadnock*
*is still there.*
*What if Monadnock*
*had moved and I*
*forgot to look?*

— Julia Older

*Grand Monadnock,*
*south side.*

109

# INDEX